20TH CENTURY SCIENCE & TECHNOLOGY

1920-40

SCIENCE FOR THE PEOPLE

20TH CENTURY SCIENCE & TECHNOLOGY – 1920-40
was produced by

David West 🛉 **Children's Books**
7 Princeton Court
55 Felsham Road
London SW15 1AZ

Designers: Jenny Skelly & Aarti Parmar
Editor: James Pickering
Picture Research: Brooks Krikler Research

First published in Great Britain in 2000 by
Heinemann Library, Halley Court, Jordan Hill,
Oxford OX2 8EJ, a division of Reed Educational and
Professional Publishing Limited.

OXFORD MELBOURNE AUCKLAND
JOHANNESBURG BLANTYRE GABORONE
IBADAN PORTSMOUTH (NH) USA CHICAGO

04 03 02 01 00
10 9 8 7 6 5 4 3 2 1

ISBN 0 431 12191 5 (HB)
ISBN 0 431 12198 2 (PB)

British Library Cataloguing in Publication Data

Parker, Steve, 1952 -
1920 - 1940 science for the people -
(Twentieth century science & technology).
1. Technology - History - 20th century -
Juvenile literature
2. Science - History - 20th century -
Juvenile literature
I. Title
609' .042

Printed and bound in Italy

PHOTO CREDITS :
Abbreviations: t-top, m-middle, b-bottom,
r-right, l-left, c-centre.

Front cover - The Kobal Collection,
Hulton Getty Collection. Pages 4, 5t, 6,
8l, 9, 15m, 21br, 22b, 24bl & br, 25
both, 26bl & br, 28, 28-29t & 29 -
Corbis. 4-5, 17b & 19b - AKG London.
5b & 22t - Vitra Design Museum. 6-7 -
Jodrell Bank Science Centre. 7t - Corbis
Digital Stock. 8r, 11, 12, 13 both, 14
both, 15t & b, 16 both, 16-17, 18 both,
19t, 21bl & 24t - Hulton Getty
Collection. 23, 26t & m & 27 - Mary
Evans Picture Library. 28-29b - Science &
Society.

*The dates in brackets after a person's
name give the years that he or she lived.*

*An explanation of difficult words can be
found in the glossary on page 30.*

20TH CENTURY SCIENCE & TECHNOLOGY

1920-40

SCIENCE FOR THE PEOPLE

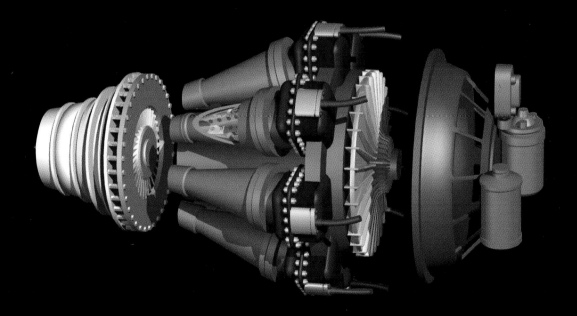

Steve Parker

Heinemann
LIBRARY

CONTENTS

In 1923 Spanish engineer Juan de la Cierva (1895–1936) devised a new type of aircraft called the autogyro. In 1928 he piloted one of his craft across the Channel (see page 17).

(see page 17).

The race to build high skyscrapers like the Empire State Building led to new construction techniques – and new dangers.

SCIENCE & POWER

During the 1920s many people in developed countries began to feel the benefits of technology and science. Electricity cables were laid into factories, offices and ordinary homes. Improved mass production methods affected almost all areas of daily life. Clothes, furniture, labour-saving gadgets, vehicles and even buildings became better yet cheaper. At the start of the 1930s the world seemed to be shrinking fast. Radio was well established and the great new wonder of the age was television. Roads were thronged with cars and trucks. Millions rode in comfort and speed on the railways, although those with more money or less time could use their rivals – passenger airlines. Research scientists probed both the tiny particles inside atoms and the vast galaxies that whirled through space. Optimism was in the air. Surely the secrets of the Universe would soon be unravelled? But towards the end of the 1930s the world was once again plunged into war. Science had played a great part in bringing prosperity and peace. Now it turned towards creating weapons of such power that the planet itself could be destroyed.

Synthetic fibres such as nylon and rayon allowed completely new types of clothing like 'nude stockings' (see page 22).

Lighter, stronger metals and plastics were used to design slimmer, more graceful products (see page 22).

DEEP SPACE

The discovery of the most distant planet of all, Pluto, and also radio waves coming from far-off stars and galaxies, showed how very tiny our Earth really is.

Jansky's work led to huge radio telescope dishes like those at Jodrell Bank, Cheshire, UK. Radio telescopes do not see light. They detect similar but much longer, invisible waves such as microwaves and radio waves, coming from objects in space.

RADIO ASTRONOMY

In 1931 American radio engineer Karl Jansky was studying natural short-wave radio sources, such as lightning bolts, that cause 'static' and interference. He noticed some weak radio waves seemed to come, not from Earth, but from the sky. More experiments showed they came from outer space – in fact, from the centre of the Milky Way. In 1933 Jansky suggested that stars and galaxies give out not only light waves but also radio waves and other types of waves, which are all forms of electromagnetic energy. This was the beginning of radio astronomy, which has told us so much about the origin and possible fate of the Universe.

From 1931 US scientist Karl Jansky (1905–50) studied natural radio waves coming from space. This equipment was at the Bell Telephone Laboratories. In 1933 Jansky discovered that the signals came from the Milky Way, our own galaxy.

In March 1930 US astronomer Clyde Tombaugh (born 1906) discovered Pluto. This dark, icy ball of rock is the smallest planet and also farthest from the Sun. No true planets have been discovered since.

HOW SMALL WE ARE!

In the 1920s US astronomer Edwin Hubble (1889–1953) greatly advanced our understanding of space. He worked at Mount Wilson's Lowell Observatory in Arizona and discovered that wispy objects deep in space, thought to be clouds of gas, were really other galaxies. Our own galaxy, the Milky Way, was only one of thousands. Hubble also noticed that light coming from farther galaxies was redder than it should be, even taking into account the effect known as red shift. This meant the farthest galaxies were moving away from each other fastest. It was excellent evidence for the idea of the Big Bang (see next page).

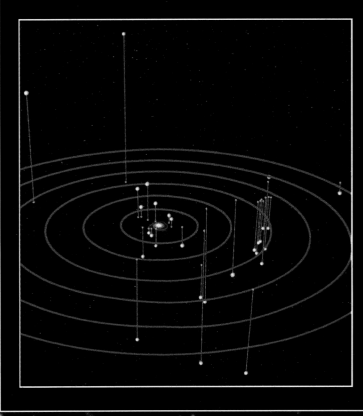

The Local Group of galaxies is shown here in relation to our own galaxy, the Milky Way, which is in the centre.

HOW WE BEGAN

As cosmologists developed Hubble's work (see previous page), the incredible vastness of the Universe became clear. At the same time fossil-hunters dug down into the past to uncover the amazing antiquity of humankind.

Fossilised skulls of 'missing links' pushed back human evolution by millions of years.

THE BIG BANG

Many astronomers followed up Hubble's work during the 1930s. It became clear that outside our own galaxy, the Milky Way, were millions more galaxies and other mysterious deep-space objects. They were so distant that light from them took billions of years to reach us. So we see these distant objects as they appeared billions of years ago. Looking into deep space is almost like looking back in time.

1949: Edwin Hubble peers through the Palomar Schmidt telescope deep into space, and also back into time.

THE BEGINNING OF EVERYTHING

The work of pioneering space scientists during the 1920s-30s is still being developed today. The Universe may be endless, but it probably does have a limited size. How can this be? Perhaps the Universe curves around and back on itself, so you can travel for ever yet never reach its edge. In 1927 Belgian astronomer Georges Lemaître proposed his 'cosmic egg' or 'primal atom' idea. This has grown into the modern Big Bang theory. All space, matter and energy came into existence in one immense explosion perhaps 12–15 billion years ago. Before this event there was nothing at all. Indeed there was no 'before'. The Big Bang was when time itself began.

2. After a few hundredths of a second the Universe has expanded to the size of the Sun.

1. Big Bang

3. After a million years the Universe continues to expand and cool. Atoms of hydrogen and helium are formed.

NO LONGER MISSING

The world was shaken in 1925 by a small fossil skull from South Africa. Known as the Taung Child, it was studied by anthropologist and surgeon Raymond Dart (1893–1988). He decided that the creature lived some two to three million years ago and it was intermediate between prehistoric apes and the humans of today – an 'ape-child'.

At the time, the idea that humans evolved from apes, or that evolution occurred at all, was the subject of great argument (see page 11). Supporters of human evolution said the Taung skull was the 'missing link'. Dart named the creature *Australopithecus africanus*. Today many experts believe that it may not have been a direct ancestor of modern humans. But it was a member of the same family and died out or became extinct.

Edge temperature persists at 1,000 billion° C

Region at some 6,000°C (about as hot as the Sun's surface)

Normal space is about minus 270°C

5. The edge of the Universe may still be expanding, with conditions there being much the same as they were in the Big Bang.

4. As the universe expands elements are formed.

9

AN UNCERTAIN WORLD
Scientists in the 1920s began to realize the world is an uncertain place. German physicist Werner Heisenberg (1901–1976) developed the uncertainty principle in 1927. It says that everything about an object cannot be known with certainty. We have to deal with what is probable or likely. The idea spread to other sciences like engineering where even new, carefully planned structures or machines are never certain to work.

The new Tacoma Narrows Bridge in Washington, USA shook itself to pieces in a light wind in 1940.

WORLD SCIENCE

One of the 'growth areas' in the scientific world during the 1930s was particle physics. Advances in very high-powered electrical devices produced so-called atom-smashing machines capable of breaking atoms into pieces. This led in turn to the creation of new substances or chemical elements for chemists to test.

NEW ELEMENTS FROM OLD

The atom-smashers such as cyclotrons worked by using electrical and magnetic energy to make atomic particles move faster and faster through long tubes. As the particles reached incredible speeds they were aimed at targets such as metals and smashed their atoms to pieces. Many particles were discovered in this way. They included the positron, a positive version of the normal electron and the first known piece of 'anti-matter', in 1932.

GAPS IN THE TABLE

The periodic table, a chart of all known chemical elements, had been known for 60 years. But the table had some gaps. Scientists believed that there were elements to fill these gaps, but they did not exist here on Earth or they were too rare here to detect.

A SMASHING TIME

In 1931 US physicist Ernest Lawrence (1901–1958) built a cyclotron at the University of California at Berkeley. Rapidly reversing pulses of electricity made a changing magnetic field which gave particles more and more energy and speed along a spiral path. Lawrence received a Nobel Prize in 1939 and element number 103 is named after him.

period 1
H	1
Hydrogen	
1	

period 2
Li	3	Be	4
Lithium		Beryllium	
7		9	

period 3
Na	11	Mg	12
Sodium		Magnesium	
23		24	

period 4
K	19	Ca	20	Sc	21		Ti	22	V	23	Cr	24	Mn	25
Potassium		Calcium		Scandium			Titanium		Vanadium		Chromium		Manganese	
39		40		45			48		51		52		55	

period 5
Rb	37	Sr	38	Y	39		Zr	40	Nb	41	Mo	42	Tc	43
Rubidium		Strontium		Yttrium			Zirconium		Niobium		Molybdenum		Technetium	
85		88		89			91		93		96		98	

period 6
Cs	55	Ba	56	La	57		Hf	72	Ta	73	W	74	Re	75
Caesium		Barium		Lanthanum			Hafnium		Tantalum		Tungsten		Rhenium	
133		137		139			178		181		181		186	

period 7
Fr	87	Ra	88	Ac	89		Ku	104	Ha	105		106
Francium		Radium		Actinium			Kurchatovium		Hahnium			
223		226		227			261		262			263

Lanthanides
Ce	58	Pr	59	Nd	60	Pm	61	Sm	62	Eu	63	Gd	64	Tb	64
Cerium		Praseodymium		Neodymium		Promethium		Samarium		Europium		Gadolinium		Terbium	
140		141		144		147		150		152		157		159	

Actinides
Th	90	Pa	91	U	92	Np	93	Pu	94	Am	95	Cm	96	Bk	97
Thorium		Protactinium		Uranium		Neptunium		Plutonium		Americium		Curium		Berkelium	
232		231		283		237		242		243		247		247	

Transition metals

Reactive metals

Inner transition metals

Poor metals

Metaloids

Non metals

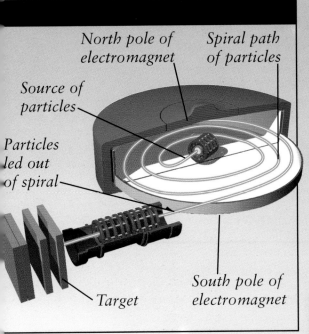

North pole of electromagnet

Spiral path of particles

Source of particles

Particles led out of spiral

South pole of electromagnet

Target

FILLING THE GAPS

In 1937 Italian–American chemist Emilio Segrè (1905–1989) used an atom-smashing cyclotron to bombard molybdenum with particles called deuterons. The result was a newly discovered element, technetium. It neatly filled a gap in the table for element 43.

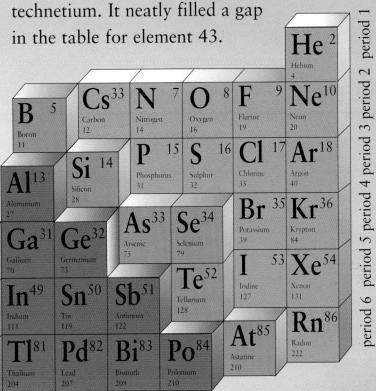

										He 2 Helium 4
				B 5 Boron 11	Cs 33 Carbon 12	N 7 Nitrogen 14	O 8 Oxygen 16	F 9 Flurine 19	Ne 10 Neon 20
			Al 13 Aluminium 27	Si 14 Silicon 28	P 15 Phosphorus 31	S 16 Sulphur 32	Cl 17 Chlorine 35	Ar 18 Argon 40

Fe 26 Iron 56 — Co 27 Cobalt 51 — Ni 28 Nickel 59 — Cu 29 Copper 64 — Zn 30 Zinc 65 — Ga 31 Gallium 70 — Ge 32 Germanium 73 — As 33 Arsenic 75 — Se 34 Selenium 79 — Br 35 Potassium 39 — Kr 36 Krypton 84

Ru 44 Ruthenium 101 — Rh 45 Rhodium 103 — Pd 46 Palladium 106 — Ag 47 Silver 108 — Cd 48 Cadmium 112 — In 49 Indium 115 — Sn 50 Tin 119 — Sb 51 Antimony 122 — Te 52 Tellurium 128 — I 53 Iodine 127 — Xe 54 Xenon 131

Os 76 Osmium 190 — Ir 77 Iridium 192 — Pt 78 Platinum 195 — Au 79 Gold 197 — Hg 80 Mercury 201 — Tl 81 Thallium 204 — Pd 82 Lead 207 — Bi 83 Bismuth 209 — Po 84 Polonium 210 — At 85 Astatine 210 — Rn 86 Radon 222

Un 109 Unnilennium

period 1   period 2   period 3   period 4   period 5   period 6

11

Dy 66 Dysprosium 163 — Ho 67 Holmium 165 — Er 68 Erbium 167 — Tm 69 Thulium 169 — Yb 70 Ytterbium 173 — Lu 71 Lutetium 175

Cf 98 Californium 249 — Es 99 Einsteinium 254 — Fm 100 Fermium 253 — Md 101 Mendelevium 256 — No 102 Nobelium 254 — Lr 103 Lawrencium 257

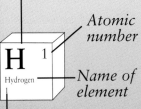

Chemical symbol (for formula)

Atomic number

H 1 Hydrogen

Name of element

Atomic mass (number of protons plus neutrons in one atom)

The periodic table arranges elements into horizontal rows or periods and vertical columns or groups. Elements in a group have similar properties to each other but are increasingly heavy. The atomic number is the number of particles called protons in the centre, or nucleus, of one atom of the element.

In 1925 school teacher John Scopes was put on trial in Dayton, Tennessee, US for teaching the idea of evolution. This showed how public pressure can suppress scientific knowledge.

FASTER AND BIGGER

At the cutting edge of technology during the 1930s were new ways of going faster and new methods of making things look bigger. The rocket engine, which first flew in 1926, was greatly improved while a new type of engine appeared, the jet. Another invention, the electron microscope, revealed tiny objects far too small to be seen with ordinary light microscopes.

ROCKET MEN

Solid-fuel rockets (as in fireworks) have been known since ancient times. US engineer Robert Goddard wanted to make a liquid-fuel rocket and reach the airless vacuum of space. His first launch was in 1926. By 1938 in Germany, Wernher von Braun (1912–1977) was building larger, faster rockets.

This scene shows the world's first successful rocket scientist Robert Goddard (1882–1945, on the far left). He is at work on a rocket with its casing removed, in about 1935. It was the year that one of Goddard's devices travelled faster than the speed of sound.

12

Combustion chamber

Fuel inlets

Exhaust nozzle

Compressor fans

THE WHITTLE JET ENGINE

A basic jet engine sucks in air, compresses it with fans, and sprays flammable fuel into it. The fuel burns in a continuous explosion and the extremely hot gases roar out of the back exhaust as a fierce stream, the 'jet'. The force of the gases blasting backwards thrusts the jet engine forwards. One of Whittle's main challenges was to develop materials that could withstand the intense heat of the explosion.

JET POWER

A jet engine is similar to a rocket but does not carry its own oxygen supply to burn the fuel, so it cannot work in airless space. British engineer Frank Whittle (1907–1996) had the idea for making a jet while he was an aero-engineer student in 1928. His first working jet, bolted to the test bench, fired up in 1937.

1948: Whittle (right) with one of his jets

Goddard's 1926 design was the first liquid propellant rocket to fly. As rockets have to be able to fly in airless space oxygen, as well as fuel, has to be carried on board. A pressurant pushed the fuel and oxidant into the combustion chamber where it was ignited to provide the thrust. This is the basic principle of all liquid fuel rockets today.

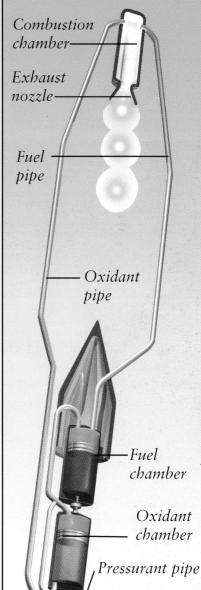

Combustion chamber

Exhaust nozzle

Fuel pipe

Oxidant pipe

Fuel chamber

Oxidant chamber

Pressurant pipe

13

By 1950 electron microscopes magnified 70,000 times and were used to study the tiniest life forms – viruses such as the flu virus.

SMALLER THAN SMALL

An ordinary microscope uses light waves to magnify tiny objects such as body cells and bacterial germs. But the length of a light wave puts a limit on magnification of about 2,000 times. German physicist Ernst Ruska (1906–1988) built a new type of microscope in 1931 which used, not light waves, but beams of electrons (as in a TV set). In 1933 his improved version magnified 12,000 times. This enabled biologists to see the smallest types of germs. Ruska was awarded a Nobel Prize for his work in 1986.

ON THE MOVE

The famous Model T Ford, the first mass-produced motor car, dominated the early years of motoring. As its production ceased in 1927, with more than 15 million built, a new wave of popular cars took to the roads. The roads themselves were improved to cope.

Percy Shaw continued to live a modest life, despite the great wealth the invention of the cat's eye brought him.

14

PEOPLE-CAR

The Model T's great successor was the German KDF, designed by Ferdinand Porsche (1875–1951) in 1934. Renamed the VW (Volkswagen) or 'People's Car', it was launched into mass production in 1938. The VW had many technical advances such as torsion bar suspension, and an air-cooled engine to cut down on the weight, expense and risk of freezing of a water-cooled system using a radiator. The VW would become the first car to reach the one-million-a-year production level, in 1962.

One of the first mass-produced Volkswagens or VWs, from 1938. It is now commonly called the 'Beetle' from its shape.

IIIA 42801

A SHINING INVENTION

In 1934 British inventor Percy Shaw (above) devised the reflective road stud or 'cat's-eye'. Driving in fog, he saw the gleam of a real cat's eyes reflected in his car's headlamps. It is said that the shining eyes made him stop just in time to avoid driving over a cliff! The cat's-eye consists of blocks of glass set into a base with a protective cover against traffic. The block's many sides are angled to reflect entering light rays straight back out in the same direction. Modern cat's-eyes are self-washing and have different colours for different road positions.

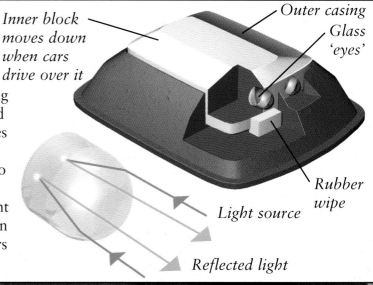

Inner block moves down when cars drive over it

Outer casing

Glass 'eyes'

Rubber wipe

Light source

Reflected light

As World War II loomed, German leaders saw that VWs could be used for military transport and so financed their mass production.

BETTER ROADS

The whole idea of the road or highway also changed. Most roads had developed from old horse and cart tracks. Germany was the first country to rethink highways as places for fast, safe, comfortable, long-distance car travel, without slow traffic turning in from small side streets. The first purpose-built wide, straight road that we would recognize as a modern highway or motorway, called an autobahn, was opened there in 1921.

ROAD SURFACE

As vehicles improved in speed and comfort, roads had to improve too. The old loose stone surface suitable for horse traffic was thrown up by car tyres. New kinds of surfacing were developed using sand, gravel and crushed stone mixed with asphalt and cement, as asphaltic concrete.

A dual carriageway motorway opens near Munich, Germany in the early 1930s.

The first long tunnel specially made for cars was the 2.6 km Holland Tunnel between New York City and New Jersey, USA, opened in 1927.

CROWDED SKIES

A great goal of long-distance travel is to cross the Atlantic Ocean between North America and Europe. In 1927 a dashing air-mail pilot amazed the world with the first solo flight.

FAST ASLEEP

The pilot, Charles Lindbergh, was financed by business people in St Louis, USA. He altered an existing air-mail plane with extra fuel tanks. The flight from New York to Paris on 20-21 May 1927 covered 5,810 kilometres and took 33 hours 29 minutes. After Lindberg had eaten his five sandwiches his main problem was staying awake!

Charles Lindbergh (1902–1974) with his heavily modified Ryan M2 aircraft, nicknamed Spirit of St Louis.

The Hindenburg *approaches the mooring mast at Lakehurst, New Jersey and turns into a horrific fireball.*

ROTARY WINGS

Many engineers have tested aircraft with wings which were not fixed but whirled around like the blades of a fan. These rotor wings created lift even when the craft itself was still, enabling it to hover. The first successful helicopter, the Focke-Achgelis FW61, flew in Germany in 1936. It reached a speed of 122 kilometres per hour.

This experimental helicopter from 1923 had four rotors turned by a central engine. The rotors were arranged in a square for stability.

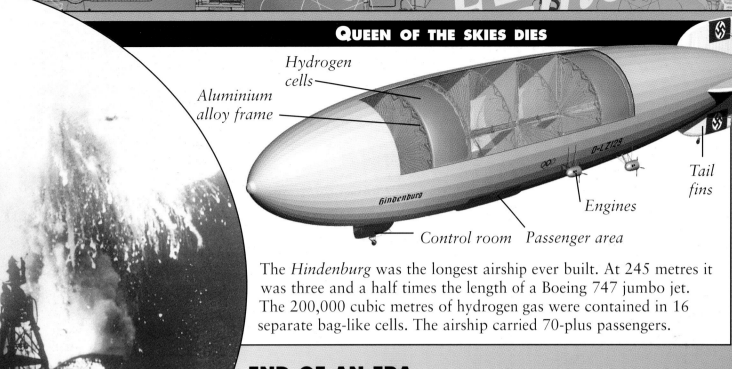

Hydrogen cells

Aluminium alloy frame

Tail fins

Engines

Control room *Passenger area*

The *Hindenburg* was the longest airship ever built. At 245 metres it was three and a half times the length of a Boeing 747 jumbo jet. The 200,000 cubic metres of hydrogen gas were contained in 16 separate bag-like cells. The airship carried 70-plus passengers.

END OF AN ERA

The first regular passenger flights across the Atlantic were not in planes but airships. Developed by the German Zeppelin Company, these massive monsters were held aloft by the lighter-than-air but flammable gas hydrogen. *Graf Zeppelin* crossed the Atlantic in 1929 with 20 passengers and 60,000 items of mail. During 1936 its sister ship *Hindenburg* carried 1,300 passengers on many regular trans-Atlantic trips. But on 6 May 1937 it burst into flames while docking in the USA with the loss of 36 lives. The disaster marked the end of the airship era.

17

In 1923 Juan de la Cierva had an idea for a new type of aircraft, the autogyro (see page 5). The front propeller was powered by an engine as in a normal plane. The rotor on top whirled around naturally in the air stream as the craft gained speed, to give additional lift.

RAILROAD FEVER

The 1930s saw the railways under great pressure. Air travel was much faster although more expensive. Trucks began to carry bulk cargo. People were becoming used to the freedom of their own cars. The railroads fought back with bigger, faster locomotives and more luxurious passenger carriages.

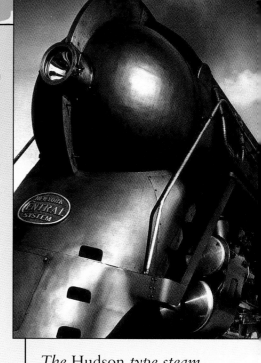

INTER-URBANS

From about 1900, especially in the USA, many large towns were connected by electric inter-urbans. These were local railways with tram-type passenger cars powered by electric motors – much like commuter railways around some large cities today. But most people did not like being tied to timetables and stations. Their new cars were much more convenient. Inter-urbans faded into disrepair.

The Hudson type steam locomotives were introduced by the American Locomotive Company in the early 1930s. By this time engineers understood the importance of streamlining for high-speed travel.

STEAM VERSUS DIESEL

As diesel engines developed in size and power they began to challenge traditional steam locomotives. Diesels were generally quieter, caused less of the obvious sooty pollution, and did not have to stop so often for water and fuel.

British steam locomotive Mallard captured the rail speed record in July 1938, at 202 km/h. The record still stands for a steam train.

18

Plane fuselage shape for locomotive

Aerodynamic scoop

THE 'PLANE-TRAIN'

In the search for greater speed and efficiency, railway technologists tried many new ideas. The *Railway Zeppelin* was an experimental locomotive built in Germany and tested in 1931. It combined various design and engineering features from railways, airships and propeller aircraft, and did away with pistons, connecting rods and other wheel-turning machinery. The scoop in the middle of the front allows the propeller to push air backwards in this region rather than blowing it against the normally blunt nose.

RISE OF THE RAILCAR

The first diesel locomotives took to the rails in 1924 in the USA – and also in Tunisia, North Africa. The diesel-electric railcar, a passenger carriage with its own diesel engine powering electric motors for the wheels, soon became popular around cities. It did not need long, expensive power lines like the electric inter-urbans.

The diesel-electric Flying Hamburger *was named after its route between Berlin and Hamburg, Germany. In 1933 it was the first high-speed railcar in regular service, with a top speed on straight track of 160 km/h.*

ON THE MAKE

During the 1920s–30s some of the greatest manufacturing advances owed their existence to new materials such as steels and other metal alloys, plastics and artificial fibres. These gave industrial engineers a whole new range of design possibilities.

THE GOLDEN GATEWAY

One of the most spectacular examples of the use for new steels was the Golden Gate Bridge over the entrance to San Francisco Bay in California, USA. Its delicate beauty made it world-famous. The project began in 1933 but hit problems with the foundations for the 227-metre-tall steel towers. One had to be set into a huge concrete block built in a coffer dam on the ocean floor. The bridge was finally opened in 1937 and carries a six-lane roadway and two footpaths. The suspension cables are 93 centimetres wide and the span between the towers is 1,280 metres.

Steel workers set up the catwalk (above left) for installing the two main suspension cables on the Golden Gate Bridge (top).

REINFORCED CONCRETE

Although reinforced concrete was first made in 1892 it wasn't widely used until the invention of the lift and the growth of skyscrapers in the 1920s. Concrete is poured into a mould with a thin steel rod framework and allowed to set. This creates a very strong and flexible structure ideal for tall buildings. It also meant architects could create buildings in any shape.

A network of steel rods is placed in a form or mould

The form is removed leaving hardened, reinforced concrete

Liquid concrete is poured in

20

HOT STRIP STEEL

Melted or molten steel can be cast into solid blocks or ingots which are then squeezed cold between massive rollers, to make long strips, beams and girders. The hot strip or continuous casting method, devised in about 1923, pushes the steel between numerous sets of rollers while it is still incredibly hot and semi-liquid. This produces longer, stronger strips.

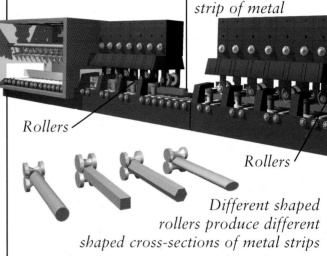

Semi-liquid strip of metal

Rollers

Rollers

Different shaped rollers produce different shaped cross-sections of metal strips

UP AND UP

Skyscrapers really got going in the 1930s as giant status symbols of success. They used steel beams and girders made by the hot strip rolling method developed in the early 1920s. In New York City the Chrysler Building became the world's tallest in 1930 at 320 metres, but only for one year. In 1931 it was overtaken by the Empire State Building at 381 metres, which held the record until 1971.

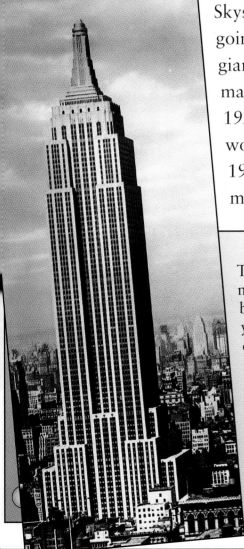

A VERY FAST BUILDING

The Empire State Building was not especially new in construction techniques. But it was built at amazing speed by 1931, in only one year 46 days. Materials were delivered daily in a 'fast-track' method. As the framework for upper storeys was being bolted and rivetted, lower floors were already finished.

The steel 'skeleton' (right) in November 1930 and the completed Empire State Building (left), 1934.

BRAND SPANKING NEW

The materials revolution of the 1930s soon spread from industry into the home. Technologists produced all manner of light yet strong substances such as steel and aluminium alloys, bakelites and other plastics, and artificial fibres like nylon and rayon. They could be moulded and shaped allowing far greater freedom in design.

The Landi chair from 1938 was made of aluminium alloy and could be left outside in the rain.

MAKING ALUMINIUM

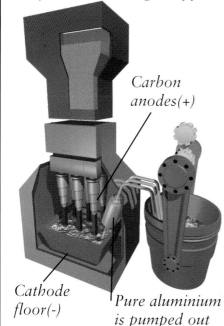

Molten alumina and cryolite are poured in through hopper

Carbon anodes(+)

Cathode floor(-)

Pure aluminium is pumped out

The shiny, silvery metal aluminium is so useful because it is very light and does not rust like iron or steel. However it is quite brittle and so often combined with other substances to form tougher alloys. Pure aluminium metal is produced in large pots or cells by the process of electrolysis. This passes a huge electric current through a mixture of cryolite and anhydrous alumina obtained from the main aluminium rock ore, bauxite.

BICYCLE TO ARMCHAIR

As with bridges and skyscrapers, the new materials encouraged much slimmer, more graceful shapes for items like furniture, cars and home appliances. In 1925 Hungarian designer Marcel Breuer (1902–81) adapted the construction of his tubular steel bicycle frame to make armchairs and other furniture. This began the uncluttered 'modernist' trend in design.

CHEMICAL COVERINGS

Raw nylon is a hot liquid that is melt-spun into fibres, as with rayon. Carothers produced it by heating adipic acid with hexa-methylene-diamine at a temperature of 270°C. In addition to fabrics, nylon's smooth hardness meant it was soon used in industry to make hard-wearing bearings and similar parts.

Nylon stockings – 'nylons'.

ARTIFICIAL FIBRE

For centuries people have used natural fibres such as cotton, wool and silk. From about 1884, chemists had experimented with a new synthetic or artificial (machine-made) fibre produced from cellulose, a major ingredient in plant matter, such as wood pulp. Methods were gradually improved with viscose rayon in 1892, to produce a fibre which could be made into cloth very similar to silk. The first rayon garments, stockings, were produced in Germany in 1910. In the early 1920s the first mass-produced clothes were fashioned from rayon fabrics, bringing the look and feel of silk (well, almost) at only about one-fifth of the price.

MORE NEW FIBRES

Synthetic fibres took another leap forwards with the invention of nylon in 1934 by US chemist Wallace Carothers (1896–1937). This followed closely his production of the first successful artificial rubber, neoprene, in 1932. Nylon, strong and smooth, was an instant hit with garment makers following its mass production from 1937. Sheer stockings made from it soon became known by its name. 1938 saw the first version of the plastic-like 'non-stick' material, teflon.

Ordinary stockings were traditionally wool or cotton to keep the legs and feet warm. In 1924 rayon stockings covered up the legs yet still allowed them to appear unclad. This daring new fashion soon caught on with the rich and famous.

MAKING ARTIFICIAL FIBRES

Nylon, terylene and similar fibres are made mainly in the chemical laboratory. They are known as polymers – long strings of identical smaller units, monomers, joined like links in a chain. A natural polymer is cellulose from plant-based matter such as refined wood pulp. This repeating structure was used to make the first versions of rayon, from the 1870s–1880s. The breakthrough came in about 1923 with innovative technology that permitted rayon's mass production from cellulose sheets.

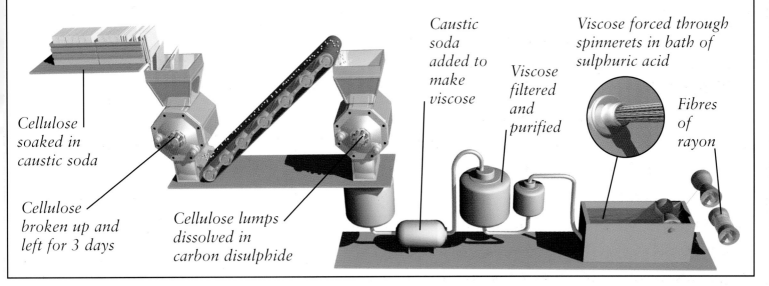

Cellulose soaked in caustic soda

Cellulose broken up and left for 3 days

Cellulose lumps dissolved in carbon disulphide

Caustic soda added to make viscose

Viscose filtered and purified

Viscose forced through spinnerets in bath of sulphuric acid

Fibres of rayon

ELEC-TECH

Many electrical machines for the office, factory and home had been invented by about 1920. The following years showed steady improvements as they became smaller, safer, more reliable and also more stylish.

LOOK, NO WIRES

The mass medium of the age was the 'wireless', or radio. The first regular radio broadcasts began in the US in 1920. In a few years most homes had a radio set. The first system was AM, amplitude modulation, where the radio waves vary in amplitude (height) to carry the coded information for sounds. In 1929 came FM, frequency modulation, where the waves vary in frequency (number per second).

Electric typewriters date from 1901. They became suitable for popular use by the 1920s. This model dates from 1925.

This 1930s radio has both AM and FM tuning bands. FM gives a clearer sound but has a more limited range.

AM · FM RADIO

MASS PANIC

The power of radio was shown in 1938 when American actor and director Orson Welles (1915–1985) read out his newly dramatized version of *The War of the Worlds* (H. G. Wells) over the radio. Thousands of people believed the Martians really were invading Earth and fled into the streets in panic.

Many people mistook Orson Welles' account of aliens from Mars attacking Earth as a true news broadcast.

THE FIRST TV

The first regular public television broadcasts, using the electronic system we have today, were made in 1936 in England. More than ten years earlier Scottish engineer John Logie Baird (1888–1946) had devised a different, part-mechanical system using a fast-spinning disc. The British Broadcasting Corporation used Baird's system for its first transmissions from 1929. But the all-electronic system replaced it in 1936.

Baird adjusts his experimental 'wireless vision' TV equipment in 1925.

1939: Baseball is shown on a General Electric television receiver. TV was truly a 'scientific wonder' at the time despite the small, blurred picture.

THE SMALL SCREEN

Television developed in stages from the 1870s, from a device called the cathode ray tube used by research scientists. In the 1920s the Russian-American physicist Vladimir Zworykin (1889–1982) worked to make a screen of many photo-electric cells, each producing an electric current related to the brightness of light falling on it. Zworykin also developed a screen with tiny dots that glowed when hit by cathode rays – which are really electron beams. These two pieces of equipment became the television camera and set.

A television uses cathode rays, which are actually beams of the negative atomic particles called electrons. These are given off by a high-voltage electron gun. Electricity passing through the focus-scan plates or coils bends the beam and makes it scan across the screen in a line, then another line below, and so on. As the electrons hit the screen they make tiny dots glow.

INSIDE A TV SET

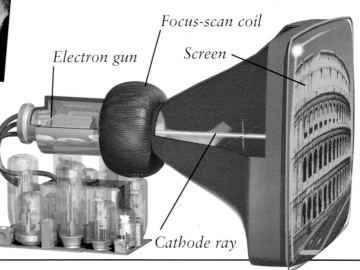

Focus-scan coil

Electron gun

Screen

Cathode ray

MEDICAL SCIENCE

MThe year 1928 saw one of the greatest of all medical discoveries. At St Mary's Hospital in London, Scottish doctor and microscope expert Alexander Fleming noticed a small round dish where he grew bacteria, moulds and other microbes ...

PENICILLIN

The dish seemed to have been contaminated by a mould (fungus) which had floated through the air and landed on it. But as the mould grew, it destroyed the bacteria around it which were supposed to be growing there. Fleming guessed that the mould produced a substance that killed the bacteria. It was called an antibiotic ('anti-life') substance. The mould was identified as a type of *Penicillium* so Fleming named the substance penicillin.

Original culture plate on which Penicillin was observed

Large penicillium colony at the top and the staphylococcal colonies around showing

Fleming's orginal dish with the mould growing at the top (large white blobs). The bacterial blobs or colonies near it have greatly shrunk.

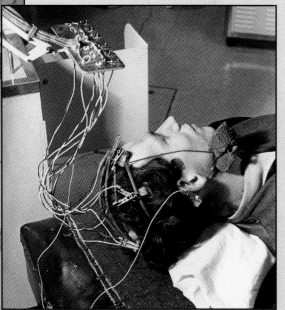

The EEG machine (electroencephalograph), which detects tiny electrical signals from the brain, was developed in 1929.

THE LIFE-SAVER

Initial tests showed that penicillin hardly harmed people, yet it killed many harmful bacteria. However it was extremely difficult to purify in large quantities for proper study. These difficulties were overcome in the late 1930s by Australian disease expert Howard Florey (1898–1968) and German-British biochemist Ernst Chain (1906–1979). In World War II penicillin was used as an antiobitic drug against wound infections and saved countless lives.

26

Alexander Fleming (1881–1955) received a Nobel Prize in 1945, jointly with Florey and Chain.

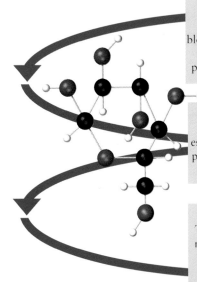

DIABETES AND INSULIN

The condition of diabetes is caused by lack of insulin, a natural body hormone that controls blood sugar. In 1921 at the University of Toronto, Canadian doctor Frederick Banting (1891–1941) and assistant Charles Best (1899–1978) managed to prepare a pure active form of insulin and save a dog with diabetes. The treatment has since saved millions of human lives.

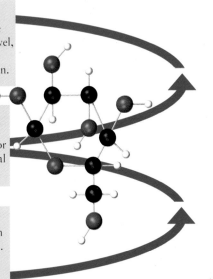

High blood glucose
Glucose passes into the blood, raising its sugar level, which stimulates the pancreas to release insulin.

Normal blood glucose
This sugar is the basic essential energy source for powering a cell's chemical processes.

Low blood glucose
This stimulates glucagon released by the pancreas. Cells lacking glucose cannot work properly.

THE FIGHT AGAINST MALARIA

The disease of malaria affects hundreds of millions of people and still causes 1–2 million deaths each year. It is due to infection with tiny one-celled organisms, plasmodia, which are spread by the bites of anopheles mosquitoes. Hopes rose in the battle against malaria with the discovery of DDT in 1939. This chemical is a powerful insecticide and kills many fly pests including mosquitoes. But in the 1950s–60s DDT was found to be very harmful to the environment and so was gradually withdrawn.

In 1923 the BCG vaccine (Bacillus Calmette-Guérin) was developed against the terrible disease of tuberculosis (TB).

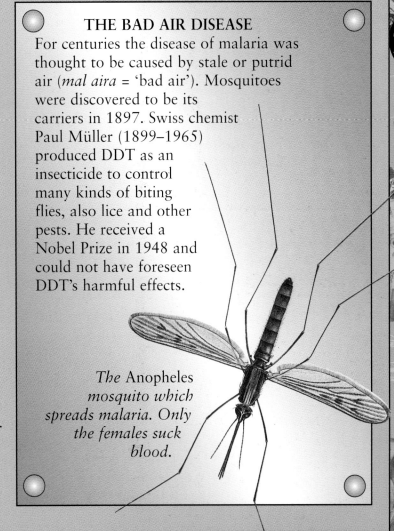

THE BAD AIR DISEASE

For centuries the disease of malaria was thought to be caused by stale or putrid air (*mal aira* = 'bad air'). Mosquitoes were discovered to be its carriers in 1897. Swiss chemist Paul Müller (1899–1965) produced DDT as an insecticide to control many kinds of biting flies, also lice and other pests. He received a Nobel Prize in 1948 and could not have foreseen DDT's harmful effects.

The Anopheles mosquito which spreads malaria. Only the females suck blood.

GADGETS GALORE

A complete list of the labour-saving gadgets and appliances developed during the 1930s–40s would fill this book. Most have faded away since they were never really useful or they have been replaced by more modern versions. However, imagine life without the ball-point pen or sliced bread.

WARNER BROS.
Supreme Triumph

AL JOLSON
in
The JAZZ SINGER

The Jazz Singer was a silent movie with music and speech added later. It used phonograph discs time-linked to the film projector.

'YOU AIN'T HEARD NOTHING YET'

These were the first words heard from the big screen at the cinema. They came from singing star Al Jolson in the movie *The Jazz Singer* (1927). This was a 'part talkie' with silent parts. The first full-length sound movie was *Lights of New York* (1928).

'BEST THING SINCE ...

... sliced bread' is one way of praising a marvellous new invention. In 1930 sliced bread was itself new. It only saved a few seconds in the time taken to find a knife and cut the loaf yourself, but it was popular from the first day. The hand-held electric carving knife arrived in 1939. (And band-aid sticking plasters at about the same time.)

One of the earliest convenience foods, sliced bread was an immediate hit.

By 1920 electric toasters had been around for some time. But the Magnet boasted extra-fast toasting.

28

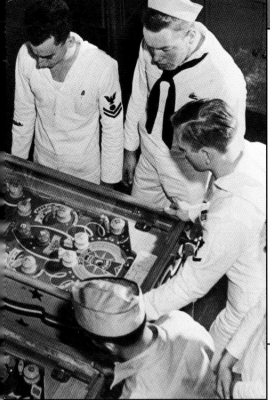

The pinball table and the jukebox were invented in the 1930s solely for pleasure. They filled in recreational time created by all the new labour-saving gadgets available.

THE WRITE-ANYWHERE PEN

Hungarian-born inventor Lazlo Biró took out a patent on the ball-point pen in 1938. It was intended for use by air crews at great height, where the low air pressure caused normal pens to flood or blob. Ball pens, often known simply as 'biros', went on sale in 1940 in Argentina. An improved version, the Reynolds model, was launched in 1945.

Pen body (barrel)

Ink reservoir tube

Brass ball socket

Porous metal ball tip

LEISURE TIME

Factories became more automated. Travel by car was faster than waiting for a bus or train. The home was full of gadgets to save time and effort. The first pre-cooked, frozen convenience foods went on sale from Bird's Eye in 1939. All these changes meant people had more time. So inventors and manufacturers devised new machines to fill it. Phonographs – record players using flat discs – became very popular, as well as radio, television and cruising through the countryside in the family car. The first tape recorders went on sale in Germany so people could store their own voices, sounds and music. It seemed that science and technology could solve almost any problem. But by 1940 the world was at war once again.

Electric razors appeared in 1931. This picture was taken by X-rays, also very popular.

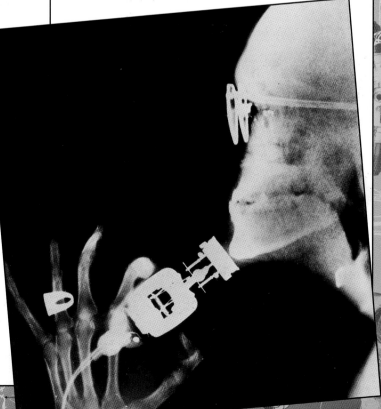

GLOSSARY

ANTI-MATTER Tiny particles of any substance that are opposites, or mirror-images, of those detected by scientists here on Earth. For example, the positron is a positive version of the usual electron, which is negative. It's thought that throughout the whole Universe, matter and antimatter balance out.

ATOM The smallest part of a pure substance (chemical element) that can exist naturally. Most atoms are made of three types of even tinier particles called protons, neutrons and electrons.

BIG BANG An event when everything began, including matter such as atoms, space and also time.

ELECTROMAGNETIC SPECTRUM A whole range or spectrum of waves consisting of combined electrical and magnetic energy. They include radio and TV waves, microwaves, infra-red, light rays, ultra-violet, X-rays (see right) and gamma rays.

ELEMENT A pure substance in which all the atoms are exactly the same. It cannot be broken apart by normal chemical methods into any other substances.

GALAXY A group of millions or billions of stars, all relatively near each other, and far away from other stars. The galaxy where our own star, the Sun, is situated is called the Galaxy or the Milky Way.

INTERNAL COMBUSTION ENGINE An engine where the fuel is burned or combusted inside a contained place, usually a cylinder, as in a petrol or diesel engine.

PERIODIC TABLE A chart of all the pure chemical substances, called elements (see left). They are arranged according to their mass (weight) and how easily they join, or combine, with other elements.

STEEL A metal substance which consists mainly of the element iron mixed with small amounts of carbon. Other elements are added for different types of steel, such as chromium for stainless steel.

X-RAYS Invisible waves of combined electrical and magnetic energy, which are part of the electromagnetic spectrum (see left). The waves of X-rays are much shorter than the waves of light. X-rays which are too powerful can harm living things.

30

WORLD EVENTS

- Women allowed to vote in US — 1
- Communist Party founded in China — 1
- Russia joins other states to become USSR — 1
- Mussolini comes to power in Italy — 1
- League of Nations gains power — 1
- Albania gains independence — 1
- General Strike in Britain — 1
- Russia: power struggle with Stalin and Trotsky — 1
- Salazar comes to power in Portugal — 1
- Term apartheid first used in South Africa — 1
- Ghandi leads protest march in India — 1
- Revolution in Spain, republic declared — 1
- Nazis take control of German parliament — 1
- Prohibition era ends in US, alcohol on sale — 1
- Long March in China led by Mao Tse-tung — 1
- Monarchy established again in Greece — 1
- Edward VIII of England gives up throne — 1
- Congress Party wins election in India — 1
- Germany and Austria join forces in Europe — 1
- World War Two begins — 1

TIMELINE

	SCIENCE EVENTS	TECHNOLOGY	FAMOUS SCIENTISTS	INVENTIONS
0	•Michelson measures the size of a star, Betelgeuse	•Regular radio broadcasts begin in US	•Bohr founds Copenhagen Physics Institute	•John Thompson devises the 'tommy' gun
1	•Banting and Best discover insulin	•The term robot first used in a play by Karl Capek	•Frederick Soddy's Nobel prize for isotope studies	•John Larson invents the polygraph or 'lie detector'
2	•Friedmann suggests the expanding Universe	•Fridges suddenly become more common in the US	•John Plaskett discovers double or binary stars	•Ice-cream is developed to become 'choc-ice'
3	•BCG vaccine developed against tuberculosis (TB)	•US radio broadcasts received in Europe	•Compton discovers the X-ray effect named after him	•Hot strip rolling of steel
4	•Edwin Hubble shows there are many galaxies	•First Chrysler cars made in US	•Oberath writes The rocket into interplanetary space	•The loudspeaker •Paper tissues – Celluwipes
5	•Robert Millikan discovers cosmic rays	•Vladimir Zworykin makes early type of TV set	•Karl Bosch invents process to make hydrogen gas	•Early types of sticky tape •Cinemascope
6	•Müller discovers X-rays can be very dangerous	•John Logie Baird tries an early version of television	•Robert Goddard launches first liquid-fuel rocket	•The first 'talking picture' movie, The Jazz Singer
7	•Georges Lemaître suggests Big Bang idea	•First accelerator or 'atom-smasher' machines	•Werner Heisenberg's uncertainty principle	•Early versions of aerosol spray cans
8	•Paul Dirac predicts the existence of anti-matter	•Radio beacons introduced for planes and ships	•Alexander Fleming discovers penicillin	•Quartz crystal clock developed
9	•Matuyama shows Earth's magnetism 'flips'	•Graf Zeppelin airship flies round world, 27 days	•Van der Graaff's high-voltage 'spark machines'	•Foam rubber (Dunlop Rubber Company)
0	•Pluto is the last true planet to be discovered	•First regular ship-to-shore radio-telephone messages	•Landsteiner wins Nobel Prize (blood group studies)	•Sound recorder with magnetic tape
1	•Linus Pauling's work on benzene chemicals	•First outside broadcast on TV, Derby horse race (UK)	•Jansky's early studies on radio astronomy	•Jacob Schick's electric razor
2	•Positron and neutron particles both isolated	•First radio telescopes constructed	•Armand Quick's Quick test measures blood clotting	•Kodachrome colour camera film devised
3	•Tasmanian wolf becomes extinct	•FM (frequency modulation) radio	•Arthur Eddington's The Expanding Universe	•Polythene developed by ICI scientists
4	•First artificial radio-active element	•Beckman's pH meter to measure acids/alkalis	•William Beebe dives to 1,000 m in bathysphere	•Reflective road stud (cat's eye)
5	•Alan Turing describes a computer by maths alone	•Watson-Watt's early type of radar in UK	•Charles Richter devises his earthquake scale	•The beer can •Technicolor for movies
6	•Oparin's 'primeval soup' origin of life ideas	•First designs for eventual VW 'Beetle' car	•Heinrich Focke's first practical helicopter	•Paperback books •Practical fluorescent lights
7	•First artificial element created, technetium	•Whittle's first working jet engine	•Hans Krebs unravels the body's cycle for use of food	•Early ballpoint pen (biro) •Polyurethane chemicals
8	•Hans Bethe suggests nuclear fusion for stars	•'Non-slip' Teflon developed	•Einstein and Infeld's The Evolution of Physics	•First photocopiers tested on the market
9	•DDT in use to kill malaria mosquitoes	•Nylon and polythene on to the mass market	•Lise Meitner introduces the term 'nuclear fission'	•Sikorsky's helicopters go on sale

INDEX